Osteology

Lizzi Hawkins

smith|doorstop

Published 2018 by
Smith|Doorstop Books
The Poetry Business
Campo House
54 Campo Lane
Sheffield S1 2EG

ISBN 978-1-912196-08-1

Designed and Typeset by Tim Morris
Printed by Biddles Books

Smith|Doorstop Books are a member of Inpress:
www.inpressbooks.co.uk. Distributed by NBN International,
Airport Business Centre, 10 Thornbury Road, Plymouth, PL6 7PP

The Poetry Business gratefully acknowledges the support
of Arts Council England.

Supported by
ARTS COUNCIL
ENGLAND

Contents

Winter Poem

The fens were frozen clean over this morning,
from the millpond out to the causeway,
where cars flow past in a way that is not unlike sleep.

I woke up at 4am, went outside and touched the frost
– you'd left the window open and I couldn't help but leave,
scrunch my toes down into the grass, observe

the gradient of the fog on the lawn, how it was almost blue.
I should have woken you, told you how close we were to snow,
that it should've rained in the night, that we could have

had that white blessing roll itself across the fields,
tug its pale hem over the city, blunting the spires,
allowing us a brief peace.

Snow is a gift – a cold measure to be held
between the tongue and the roof of your mouth
when breathing, or rolled up into ice

on the palm. We could do with a gift
right now, could do with being bundled up and held
by the whiteness, could do with our voices

being taken away, so that we cannot say these
hurtful things any longer.

Osteology I

A love poem to the engineers tunnelling under London,
sounding out the city's weight with drills
and flashlight Morse:
                    I've learnt the way the rocks must first
be read like the body, with an x-ray machine, how the cables
bring back the answer from the dark

here, the fault lines and breakages –
the places where you must take care

Kissing the Geographer

was best. His mouth folded up
like two ox-bow lakes put together.
He touched my neck and said
it was the white of a coastal stack.

The geographer would comb my hair out
and wade in it like water –
he had hands that had known riverbeds,
the innards of a seismometer trace.

On weekends, the geographer liked to go out
into the country with a compass
and the latest OS. He would say:

I'm just old school like that, baby

and flip his hair like a horse.
I'd turn off my phone GPS to make
the experience more enjoyable for him.

He'd unfold the map on his bonnet,
circle landmarks with a biro,
trace the local river back through its tributaries,
often hold my hips, find the source in my mouth.

Church

The inside of the church like the belly
of a whale: high, white bones,
and the candles' pale, unsteady fingers –
the dark pool of pews.

It has been so long since this:
the unlocking of throats for the anthem,
the priest raising his hands as if
in the conjuring of a beast.

*Sometimes to be spat out is to be given
new life,* he says,
and I think –

if we could only all be Jonahs,
roll out of the darkness
and onto a beach somewhere,

shrug off the memory of the heavy things,
wake up to sunlight
and one cheek frosted in sand.

I leave the church early,
with the buses on Hills Road lit up like Christmas
and *The Body of Christ keep you in eternal life,*

and later, your hand on my belly
in the dark, and the dark of the bed
like an ocean, and the smell of incense
in my hair, and your stark
white backbone.

Tell me if this isn't true:
that we are all just trying to stay warm
in these cold and difficult times.

Osteology II

The boys on the roof,
and the late morning,
the sky's white envelope

waiting to be cut.
The building going up now at two
or more floors a day.

All I can think about is you,
and all the reasons
you cannot stay put in this city,

all I can watch is the speck of a man
in the crane's control box,
guiding the counterweight
to lift great concrete panes –

the construction a slow
metal unfolding, an unshrugging,
the steel glint of I-beams,
the sigh of hoisted glass

Jebel Hafeet

At the top of the mountain
we stop in a layby, and buy watermelon juice
to cool the backs of our throats.

We can only touch the car now
with sleeves folded over
our hands – it's that hot –

and I can't take off my sunglasses
without wincing at the glare
like someone's put a lamp right up to my eyes.

There's a playground, two restaurants,
and a villa crouched on the yellow peak
with four security checkpoints

up the drive. You suggest that
this is where the Sheikh lives –
on the country's top shelf –

and I say *no, this is where the sun
lives* – never in anything's shadow.
I read the visitors' map, like always,

and you throw rocks over the carpark railings,
and we are both surprised when the clatter
of stone on stone doesn't come.

When we pool our coins to buy plastic
rings from a repurposed bubblegum machine
and I get down on one knee,

you drag me up by the wrist and tell me that *it's not funny,*
this is the kind of shit that'll get you arrested here,
but you still hold my hand all the way home,

even when you change gears,
even when I'm wiping sand out of my eyes,
even when, on the 16-lane highway,

we have to call the cops twice
to report a man who's been hit by a car,
and you cry all the way home

because you say that the man carrying him off the road
was probably the one who hit him,
and carrying wasn't what he was doing.

The Hunt

It starts with my father,
who wants to see fox-hunting legal.
We agree to disagree
but I can't shake the thought,

and later, when we talk of matadors,
the understanding slides into place:
how very estranged we are
from death, now, and mostly thankful,
but that some men will give chase
on horseback, with hounds,
with a desperate red silk
just to look it in the teeth.

Perhaps it is that distant things
become the most desirable,
for example how many boyfriends
of friends have asked
to choke them during sex.

Or worse:
a red inheritance, wedged
in our chests; the unspeakable
capabilities of the body,
to be held down,
to be kept far from the heart.

Poem for Flora

And so the storm broke
at 11 o'clock last night.
We were sat in the bus station,
watching the clouds pour
themselves out of the sky, and you
asked me why I never write poems
about you. You didn't understand
we've been writing our own poems for years,
that it's all we've ever really done,
that we'll do it again, in a few hours' time,
driving home in one of your cars,
with the roof down, standing
up on the back seats,
wind making shining slipstreams
of our hair and clothes,
watching the bypass lights turn to blurs
above our heads.

In Praise of Geologists

who give us the lollipop words:
gabbro, bauxite,
the joy of rolling *car-bor-un-dum*
out across our lips.

It is for you that absent-minded beachcombers
fill their pockets with purple slate
and lay it down on their doorsteps
like semaphore.

For geologists:
who read the slow language of granite,
who core ice like apples,
who offer up agates, sliced into Saturn's rings –

Give us again the blasted rain cups of quarries,
narrate the red moonscape of an open-cast mine.

Surely you are the patron saints of boy scouts,
of beaming girls scrambling
up scree with bloody knees –

for who has not found joy in the smooth,
overflowing handfuls of pebbles
that only oceans can give us,

the glassy winnings of clinking fistfuls of quartz.

For geologists, who dance to the beat of their
own drum
like we may only dare,
a drum that beats with every geomagnetic
hitch –

Praise, then, geological time,
the tidy extrusion of it like Battenberg,

Precambrian, Gelasian, Quaternary, Miocene,

stacking up behind us, O
how we wish we could be laid out
like that, have you read us
by our stony, bent backs.

After the Forecast

Finally, we woke to snow,
creaking in the silver-birch trees
in the garden,

piled, like cream, on the window ledge,
two foot up the front
and patio doors.

Both cars unmoveable – and us
shipwrecked in the living room,
in onion-layers of fleeces and socks,

acting out
any number of emergency
callout ads.

Strange, that it is so easy,
in the snow, to take another life
and wear it like a coat.

That there's such ease
in towns sealing up,
along the boundaries of rivers,

and previously arterial roads.
Our unexpected desire:
to live sparsely,

to shrug on the ways
of our great-greats,
to be like the shepherds

I read about somewhere,
who didn't come down
from the Dales til the 20s,

unable to decipher all
but the speech of their herd.
I boil milk on the gas

in the kitchen,
and my mother
comes in from hacking

ice from the birdbath,
and we are
stilled, in the frost,

unrequiring of language
– mouths closed to keep
in the warm,

hands fixed on the metal
pan, the spinning galaxy
of stirred milk.

Train

The crows are lifting off like black film, peeling.
I haven't spoken to you in person for four days now.

The train goes past a yard of sheet metal
and a postage depot and I can't work out

if I'm emptying out or filling back up
with all of these cities at the same time

it's all of these cities and the lack of stopping
Manchester is a spreading pool in the distance.

It is really a corkscrew in my chest now
I miss my home and my other home.

Bradford did you miss me you're a steely husband
with filter paper in your teeth.

Bradford did you miss me no wait don't answer the question.
When I came home yesterday I was almost shaking

and the sensation hasn't yet gone.
I took a bath and the storm grabbed the window

almost off its hinges.
The wind is a warning I can't stop thinking isn't a warning.

I can't stop thinking about a boy with fat white fingers
and a house on Lensfield Road.

I feel that I've been tapped like a tree
and it's all coming out.

If I were an oak tree I'd have green under my fingernails
and schoolgirls would light up underneath me on rainy afternoons.

When we went over the canal I wondered about locks
how many men it took to lift the water over the Pennines,

all that weight on their backs.
This cold country is ungrateful for our labours,

we should take off somewhere else and be trees together.
I haven't been home in a while now and I think it would be nice

I haven't been home in a while now I miss
my bedsheets, the way light pools

behind my curtains as if it is waiting to touch me.
I know you've been waiting to touch me

but I've been ignoring your phone calls and text messages.
I've been waiting to touch someone else, I don't know if you're aware.

There's four hours of safe distance between us
that's not enough that's far far too much.

I should like to peel myself out of all of this like a bird
and go back to my parents' house.

Osteology III

a boy on Blackfriars bridge
                              arms out ready to take flight into
the Thames
                    a flock of pigeons
                                        a group of girls with their ankles bare

here in the medical school we are studying haemoglobin

the way water moves across a gradient
                                        and leaves the blood
the city in November is grasping
                              the cold again
                                              coming home
to the blinds open
                              and no light on the kitchen table
no light through the bus windows
                              these overcast mornings
no light
                    on the chopping board or when I stand over the sink

Mercury Invents the Alphabet

in the year 400 BC, watching
a flock of cranes.

The Aegean is a marble in the afternoon's
hot mouth, and the cranes are sudden

thunder, unfurling
on an updraught,

scrolling their bodies into
letter-like shapes,

electrical: the motion
of wings.

And not unlike a thunder strike,
this new potential for speech –

rolling in, as it does,
from the sea.

Cranes, native to the east,
now present in southern Greece,

and the boys dropping pebbles into the sea,
unaware of the flight overhead,

the white herd, agitating.
What shocking clarity

of bodies, of language
being made in the shapes

of birds, that this
strange pale flock

could find voice in the
angling of shoulders,

the grace and flex of the neck.

Peaks

1. Ingleborough

The first vision is the right one:
the green shrug of the hill. A pair of shoulders,
where the ground has cracked its back
and made to rise where it can,
and before this, the flat hand of the village, the caves,
the cleavage of rock giving up the higher land.

From here you can see the west coast,
the drowning-trap of Morecombe Bay
   where the tide coming in will outrun a horse
and after the sand, where the sea is the blue rim
of a bowl.

I love it here best in the winter,
when the farmers burn patches of heather
to let through new shoots,
and the hillside goes up in flares against the grey –

how strange it must be to inhabit the valley,
for the cold months here to be so untame.
For winter to carry not only frost,
but flame.

2. Pen-Y-Ghent

This time, we go up in March, on the cusp
of the Easter break. The ascent is a long overtaking –
teenage boys with rucksacks and no cagoules,
old couples with gaiters and spiked walking poles –
all pass us. We take time, take in the quarry
cut from a nearby fell, the crease
of train tracks on the valley floor.

The hill is a curved tongue, at the top
it is both hands to stone, each hold the silvered back
of a funhouse mirror. Hard to understand:
the time, the hundred perfect horseshoes scooped away
only by palms and the soft percussion of rain.
Instead, I imagine the impossibility of hooves,
and the rock coming away with
the thickness and softness of cake.

3. Whernside

Not yet walked,
the final peak.

Still unbagged, and its invitation
slung out to the west side,

as if it is waiting for us.
One day we will go up

and find the county border
that runs the summit cheek to cheek,

cross into Cumbria to lay our hands
on the trig point. Say our grace:

for the good days, the days where fog
was a hood, rising, the days when the route

was clear, the days where we were
granted passage, round every switch

of the path, so that we could always
keep on walking.

Constellations

It's not often that the sky is clear
round here (or that the afterglow of cities
doesn't drown the stars),
but when it is,
and the mood takes him,
my father huddles on the patio
in his dressing gown
and deciphers the sky for me.

The Pleiades, Betelgeuse, Cassiopeia, Charon:
We pass these to each other like sweets
and trace the cupped hand of the Plough,
turning our heads up,
finding the white necessity
of the pole star.

This is the brittle language that we speak in,
constellations, the bright clouds of nebulae,
moments where everything seems
at touching distance.

Calcium

is the twentieth element in the periodic table,

sits at the top of the reactivity series,
is what your bones are made of.

Calcium is the reason for the gleaming white quick of your teeth,
the skeleton paleness of coral reefs.

When the Fibonacci coils of shells
shelve off the coast, it is in a slow love
of minerals that Calcium is crystallised and compressed
to make gaping strata of limestone

that will rear up later as chalk land,
valley-mouths, hills that show through their finger bones.

In the south, men have carved great horses
into the sides of these hills,
that flail their hooves
and shriek their whiteness to nobody.

Look, they are flexing and arched
like truths that time casts uncomfortably.

Look, look, they are older than what makes them,
like poems, like gospel,

your bones outlasting you.

Wharfe Valley

We've been waiting for snow for a week now,
have stopped being able to look out of windows,

bring ourselves to step onto pavements
or set foot in the garden without wondering how

these things will feel under the white hand of frost,
how our human warmth would mar the lacework

at a touch. Yesterday I took washing off the line
and felt it bite like steel in my fingers.

Gritters are leaving their trails in the road every evening,
like a message to the cold, and coming down through the valley

you can see the grey slice of the Wharfe, tight and waiting
for the push into ice. This morning across the table I said

I thought the sky looked like it was holding its breath
and when it let go we'd get snow clouds,

billowing. Coming back off the hills afterwards
I caught the shriek of the wind in my coat sleeves

and took splinters from black ice with my bicycle tyres.
We have started leaving our doors open in hopes

the snowdrifts will not be able to resist us.
We are all waiting for the cold to close its open fist.

Acknowledgements

My thanks to the editors of the following publications, in which some of these poems first appeared: *The North, Ambit, The Compass Magazine, Introduction X,* and *The Rialto.* Thanks also to *The Cadaverine,* and East Leeds FM for publishing and broadcasting my early work, and to Arvon, at whose Word Exchange residential this pamphlet was completed.

I owe a huge debt of thanks to Steve Dearden and The Writing Squad for all the mentoring, support, and opportunities they have given me. Particular thanks are also due to Helen Mort, whose feedback was invaluable in writing this pamphlet, and to Danny Broderick, for critiquing many of these poems in their earlier forms.

I am grateful to Ilkley Literature Festival for all its support, and to all the members of the Ilkley Young Writers group for their friendship and critique over the years. Special thanks to Becky Cherriman and Michelle Scally Clarke, who were the most inspiring tutors I could ever have asked for, and without whom I would not have pursued poetry in the way that I have. Finally, thanks to my family, for their love and unwavering support in everything that I do.